Just Being

Joanna Button

I'd like to thank my mother, Susan Kay, and a close family friend, Selma McLaren, for assisting me with the editing of this book. Many thanks to my mother, Robert Lee, and to Rebekah Tazewell for providing the images.

First published by Joanna Button, 2021
Copyright © Joanna Button, 2021

The moral right of the author has been asserted.

All rights reserved. Without limiting the rights under copyright reserved above, no part of this publication may be reproduced, stored in or introduced into a retrieval system, or transmitted, in any form or by any means (electronic, mechanical, photocopying, recording or otherwise), without the prior written permission of the copyright owner.

National Library of Australia
Cataloguing-in-Publication data:
Button, Joanna, 1974-
Just Being.
978-0-6450941-0-7 (pbk)
978-0-6450941-1-4 (ebook)
1. Spirituality. 2. Self-actualisation (Psychology).
3. Happiness. I. Title.

Dragonfly image by Rebekah Tazewell, Tazewell Photography.
Photo of Joanna and dogs at Floriade 2019 by Robert Lee.
Photo of Joanna and dogs on the beach taken by Susan Kay.

Book prepared for publication by OdysseyPublishing.com

Contents

Introduction	1
My Life Story	6
Step Up or Step Off	14
Universal Principles on the Natural Order/ Power of Energy	17
Individual Preferences to Spirituality and Religion	26
Connection through Universal Love	28
Negativity Trend Developing	30
Technological Advancements – More of a Hindrance	34
Basis of Meditation	37
Can Women Have It All in This Day and Age?	40
Relationships Today	46
Rewiring Our Mind and Overcoming Addictions/Unproductive Behaviour Patterns	48
We Can Heal Ourselves	51
No Such Thing as 'Death'	57
Integrity and Resilience	59
References	61
About the Author	64

Introduction

How much pain and suffering can humanity endure before we realise that we are not living on this planet the way we are meant to? Humans are more powerful than we realise. However, we have to learn to quieten our minds and control our thoughts to harness this power. Collectively, we have created our existence on this planet and we are responsible for the developments arising in this world. As creators of our destiny, we choose the way we live through our thoughts and actions!

Every one of us is special, unique, and here for a purpose. We are intended to live in harmony with nature and to work cooperatively with all living things as part of one universal whole. Humans have created a lot of distractions that do not serve us now, nor will they in the future. Humanity's survival depends on us becoming more conscious of our impact on our environment and the living things within it. There is an urgency to change our destructive ways, as we are causing irreparable damage to our world.

As children, we are brought up according to society's conditioning and simply accept as truth what we are taught by our parents and at school. We are taught right from wrong, which is questionable, as not even the Source (equivalent to the Creator, God, or higher power) itself would place such value judgements on our behaviour. As we are all made from the same energy as the Source, we are here to experience the Source itself, and without contrast, opposites, and diversity this would not be possible.

I was brought up believing that I would attain happiness if I applied myself at school, secured a good job, bought a house, got married, and gave birth to children. I feel like I have been sold a lemon; I was a very good student, and after pushing myself so hard to achieve three of the 'happiness requirements', this teaching simply did not ring true for me. The catalyst for my awakening was when I travelled to Africa in 1995 to discover that the children there, materially poor, were more spiritually rich than I was. 'The greatest wealth is to live content with little' (Plato). Western society has lost something essential: our sense of community spirit.

As a communications professional, I have learned that there is no 'silver bullet' when it comes to ensuring a message is perceived as it was sent, and in this age of information overload, it is difficult to cut through all the noise, distractions, and misinformation. It is also concerning to learn that our perception of the same message depends on our individual makeup, including our cultural background, educational level, language skills, gender, and religion, to name a few. There can be many versions of the same truth and, consequently, people's perceptions form their reality. 'All that we are is the result of what we have thought' (Buddha).

As humans, by our very nature, we will unfortunately never be able to develop systems that apply fairly, justly, and perfectly to all involved. Take our legal system as an example; it does not always serve to protect the victim. For example, there have been times where the accused was treated as guilty before the outcome of the judicial process, or where the 'court of public opinion'—through what's aired in the media—prejudices the outcome of legal proceedings.

It's therefore extremely comforting, and even makes it bearable for me to live in this world we've constructed, to know that there are inescapable universal principles that apply equally to us all: karma! In reality, there is only one universal TRUTH. And we all inherently know it! Whether people see the truth depends on how aligned they are with the natural order.

It is disheartening to witness so many humans suffering because they are unaware of the existence of the natural order. The 'power of energy' states that we attract back to us whatever we put out into the universe. Without knowing any better, we have adopted our forefathers' unfounded teachings. By 'forefathers' I mean the 'cultural (especially male) ancestors of past generations who have originated or contributed to a common tradition or idea shared by humans' (yourdictionary.com).

We all have a right to happiness, peace, and contentment, without pressure to define and distinguish ourselves and compete with one another for what is believed to be 'scarce' resources. With the Source, everything is abundant and possible; however, humans struggle to comprehend this with our limited minds.

Living as 'spiritual beings' in our human form in this lifetime will also ensure that humans feel a sense of belonging and a higher purpose. Each of us fits into a much larger macro picture as well, which is currently unfolding. We all have a role to play as part of the 'collective' too.

"This above all, may thy own self be true" (Dead Poets Society)

*as when you find your true self, you find true love.
Because they are the same.*

My Life Story

I was brought up believing that I needed to focus on school and my studies to gain the job I wanted. This would result in security and success and ultimately lead to happiness. I do not know anyone my age who has completed more work and study than I did up until the age of forty. For nine years, I worked full-time while studying part-time to complete my undergraduate degree, graduate certificate, diploma, and then master's degree. I ended up becoming a professional in the field of communication and media and was able to put these qualifications to good use through opportunities working for the Australian Government (a very secure position to have).

My career took centre stage when I started working for the Department of Defence in 2002. Working as a media adviser to the head of an organisation saw me develop as a communications professional. I had always given 110 per cent to my work, as I did with my studies, and had been thorough, but the volume of work started to exceed the capacity of one person. While I would attempt to promote good news stories on behalf of my organisation, it was the 'hot issues'—deaths, accidents, and misbehaving military members—that took up most of my time. In addition, I had to deal with politics, red tape, bureaucracy, and other frustrations at play—just the nature of working in the public sector.

I was paid to be on-call 24 hours a day, seven days a week, to uphold my organisation's reputation and to better serve the 24/7 news cycle. Someone in this position is almost set up to fail from the start, with the expectation that one person can solely manage and uphold an organisation's reputation when so many things can contribute to it. Interestingly, my experience as a Defence Media Adviser guided the graduate teaching and theory at Charles Sturt University at the time, as Defence was seen as cutting-edge. Wars are conducted 24 hours a day, with coverage being transmitted into people's lounge rooms instantaneously. Defence needs to respond promptly to round-the-clock media enquiries, especially about tragedies involving Australian Defence Force members. Also, Defence needs to respond in a timely fashion to an enemy who is increasingly using digital communication to spread their messages and propaganda.

Through this experience, I gained a real insight into both the news-making cycle and the workings of the government. Let me just say, perceptions are indeed reality. This is why I am passionate about communication. I was a strong supporter of Freedom of Information and totally against any form of censorship. I believed that information should be accessible to all, with all given an equal voice and publishing rights.

This was until I understood the power of energy.

I have come to believe that misinformation can be more damaging to our spiritual beings than no information at all. In fact, there is way too much information!

It does NOT serve us as spiritual beings to give any of our energy to anything negative unless that's what we want to attract back. How does it serve humankind to have recordings of beheadings or 'how to make bomb' instructions freely available on the Internet? Even if you continue to knowingly watch negative segments such as the daily news, you are contributing to this global problem rather than to its solution.

As negativity attracts more negativity, the number of catastrophes, crises, deaths, and murders will continue to grow and become more extreme until we reverse this trend. As all living things are connected, no individual can escape the impact.

The increasing severity of these events will result in them becoming less palatable to the public. Hopefully, this will lead to more people becoming awakened, as they question the truth behind these increasingly unacceptable 'created realities'. More people will realise that what's portrayed in the media doesn't accurately represent what they know to be true. The content of news disseminated through the mass media should be at least balanced with equal air time given to positive stories.

We need to be mindful of putting harmless information out there too, as it all serves to distract people from going within and discovering the universal truth. Each person thinks thousands of thoughts per day and those thoughts can be divided into five categories including: (i) negative thoughts (toxic); (ii) waste thoughts (unproductive thoughts about the past or future); (iii) necessary thoughts (neutral but needed to perform daily tasks); (iv) positive thoughts (affirmations); and (v) elevated thoughts (higher quality). Elevated and positive thoughts are light in nature and produce positive action, whereas negative and waste thoughts lead to mental fatigue and leave us feeling deflated. We need to understand the quality and impact of our thoughts before we verbalise them, especially when you consider that humans spend 95 per cent of their day on unproductive thoughts about the past or future.

People are better guided from the Source within rather than following external influencers. If everyone lived according to the power of energy, our current global problems would cease to exist. It is not for humans to judge whether information is harmless, informative, or educational. Whether people are exposed to censored information is irrelevant, as once a thought has been conceived, it can manifest itself in our future. Filtering uncontrolled content will not prevent harm to readers.

None of my messages are new, as you will see from the selection of quotes/sayings included throughout this book. In this book, I propose a set of universal principles that taught me how to find a constant state of peace and contentment. I wish that I had been given these principles as a child as a sort of mantra to live by. I never knew how loved we all are, as we are all part of the same energy source as the Creator! We are here to *experience* life as free, spiritual beings and our human form enables us to *perceive* this experience.

Until I attained this learning, I felt insecure and anxious, feeling immense pressure to meet society's expectations and prove my worth. I'd argue that I felt the growing tension between my parents before I even entered this world, because becoming conscious of the impact of our behaviour was a lesson I needed to learn in this lifetime.

Born in 1974, I grew up before my time as the eldest of two siblings. With similar characteristics to my father, I felt equipped to deal with his angry and controlling tendencies, more so than my mother, who is loving, innocent, and trusting. While my parents did the best they could at that time, our family life was challenging. I was six years old when my parents divorced. While my mother had primary care of my brother and I, we stayed at my father's house every second weekend. I never felt content and complete within myself, which was only exacerbated by going between two homes throughout my childhood.

It's difficult to feel inner peace and harmony when you're in fight-or-flight mode. Even if you sense a warning of possible danger, you choose how to respond. Our society tends to reward the victim, which is evident with the saying, 'the squeakiest wheels get the most oil'. Even our insurance policies operate from a place of fear by compensating the victim in the event of an accident, incident, or injury. We need to be careful as these practices are inconsistent with the power of energy, which rewards those individuals who serve and give to others. 'I never saw a wild thing sorry for itself. A small bird will drop frozen dead from a bough without ever having felt sorry for itself' (D.H. Lawrence).

I do not claim that all of the universal principles I've devised are entirely correct. I've tried to express these principles simply to cater for the lay-person. For some readers, these will serve to reinforce their prior knowledge, while others will require more information. To assist with this, I've tried to develop and contextualise the concepts under the sub-headings that follow.

I offer these universal principles to challenge the 'status quo' and invite anyone to test these as I've done. I warmly welcome debate on these higher-level thoughts, as I believe these are what matter in this life and beyond.

Through harnessing the power of energy, for example, I consistently find I can attract a vacant car park. While travelling to my destination, I verbally express gratitude to my angels, believing I've already received the car park. The more a person expresses gratitude for what they expect, the more it will manifest itself in their life. The Source takes care of the 'how'; we just need to be clear on what we expect and express our gratitude for it. If one person can 'free' up a car park, imagine what a group of like-minded individuals could achieve if all are focused on a common goal and mindful of the natural order.

There is much work to be done. Once people have tested the principles to validate their existence, the next challenge lies in ensuring that our lifestyle choices, educational systems, cultural practices, technologies, and architecture all better serve us as spiritual beings. While it seems insurmountable, each person can only change themselves and life will become easier to live when aligned with the natural order.

If this book inspires just one person to question their conditioning and their enduring values and beliefs, then it will have been worth my effort. The Source will ensure that this book reaches those who are ready to receive it. For those who would like to live life as nature intended, I'm here and waiting. 'Nice of you to have shown up!'

*"Whatever our situation,
it is important to realise that we
are infinitely more than even our
greatest achievements."
(Hamilton, The Magic of the Moment)*

Step Up or Step Off

This is an urgent call to action, as we are not living on this planet the way nature intended. If it is not nature's way—and this is something we have all been programmed with—then it is simply not going to serve the planet. There is a fragile balance that exists between all living things, which is guided by the power of energy.

We should not be living like this … and we all intuitively know it! Why choose to suffer in denial, when we can awaken to the truth and live our heaven peacefully here on Earth? It's time to wake up, humans, as we have not only failed in our caretaker responsibilities, we are effectively destroying the planet and everything in it.

Humanity is a collection of individuals. As we have all contributed to this age-old problem, it requires a collection of us to bring about the profound cultural change needed for our species' survival.

Be conscious of your impact on the environment and other living things, or cease being, as to exist in suffering is only harmful to yourself and other living things around you. It's time to stop overlooking the signs and living such a destructive lie. Our collective reality is not marrying up with what we know to be the truth. We are all inherently good and loving, so it's time for each of us to be true to ourselves in order to solve this global problem.

According to karma, we have to make up for mistakenly following the fears experienced in our human form, instead of being guided by the sacred programming that resides within each of us. Our fears have been conditioned within us: of not being accepted, of not meeting society's expectations, of being broke, overweight, or alone. When we consider that all living things make up an equal part of the same complex, interconnected whole, it is inconceivable how humans have conducted themselves throughout history with such a sense of entitlement and superiority.

The natural order ensures that these unfounded actions adopted from our forefathers will only result in our decline and eventual extinction. We are sabotaging ourselves. The Source intended for us to live as happy, free, spiritual beings, so it is disturbing that we have constructed realities that lessen our sacred guidance and confine our ability to do just that. Unless it abides by the natural order, we shouldn't impose anything such as economy, work, laws, rules, or capital punishment, or it will only be to our detriment.

There is nothing new in the messages contained in the universal principles outlined below. In fact, some of the messages have been stated previously by a famous philosopher. However, I have tested and proven each of these principles, as they were essential learnings for me to discover my true identity and to achieve a sense of peace after struggling for much of this life. I'm interested in attempting to make people feel better within themselves and invite anyone interested to challenge these principles, as I have done.

"Built the train tracks over the Alps between Vienna and Venice before there was a train that could make the trip. They built it anyway ... they knew the train would come one day."
(Under the Tuscan Sun, 2004)

Universal Principles on the Natural Order/Power of Energy

Whether you believe in these principles or not, this is the way the world and our lives unfold. Regardless of whether you're in your ego or spiritual state (or in your spiritual being or human form), all life abides by these universal principles, which are equivalent to spiritual laws. You cannot escape them! It is the natural order of things. These principles apply across all forms of religion, spiritual beliefs, and whether you're enlightened/awakened or not.

- All living things are made up of the same energy as the Source, and all living things vibrate at different frequencies. The Source is equivalent to the Creator, God, higher power, universal love, and our eternal true selves—which is all energy.
- All living things are born with inherent value and we are all equal. I see myself as equal to a blade of grass! You do not need to 'do' or achieve anything to gain value, and nor do you need to be defined, identified, or distinguished.
- All living things are 'connected' by the same universal source. This 'oneness'/connection between all living things is through this energy. While all living things are part of the same universal whole, we are all unique and all have a unique contribution to make.

- We are here to experience the diversity of human behaviour as spiritual beings. Do not be fearful, as if you work with the Source you will only attract experiences that you can overcome.
- We are creative spiritual beings, only limited by our human mindsets. Whatever we think today will manifest itself in our future. We are what we think! So, if you don't like something in your life, change the way you think. We create our reality by displaying today the qualities we would like to manifest in our future.
- 'Start the way you would like to finish.' This is about the management of our expectations and recognising the power of the mind. It is also about taking care of yourself first so that you *can* assist others.
- If what you're trying to change doesn't come naturally, you must be disciplined, show faith, and take corrective action—without just seeking instant gratification—to develop mind-muscle (new behaviour patterns).
- Humans, like all living creatures, are inherently loving and compassionate and should take only what we need for survival. To say that humans' inherent nature is competitive, aggressive, violent, and negative is a misconception adopted by our forefathers.
- Humans have become too greedy and unconscious of our footprint on this planet. In nature, most wild animals live together harmoniously and only take/kill what they need to live.
- Karma is balanced in all directions in the fullness of

time. Karma may be positive or negative and is not for humans to judge. The fewer emotional attachments humans have, the fewer 'karmic opportunities'—both good and bad.

- You cannot change the situation; however, you can control your response to it.
- Your behaviour is your karma; another's response is their karma. Accept it!
- Take responsibility for all your actions, thoughts, and feelings—all living things 'sense' all that is put out into the universe. We attract back what we put out! Anger especially multiplies. Western society is trending toward manifesting increasingly more negativity.
- Through applying these universal principles, you are fully present in the moment, allowing you to transcend time and space. When you are truly present in the moment, you do not want for anything, nor do you have any immediate problems. The power is in the 'now'! (Tolle 2004).
- Life is about your personal journey, with the most important thing being how you feel about yourself, rather than whether you're meeting society's expectations or gaining others' approval. So, your personal journey is about true self-knowledge/self-awareness. It should be an inspiration, which may result in self-improvement (you decide) and change in others (bonus).
- You can only change yourself. Accept others as they are; you cannot change them.

- No person, place, or thing has any power over you (unless you allow it!). 'Control your own destiny or someone else will' (Jack Welch, General Electric). You are responsible for your happiness. Take ownership of your own issues only.
- Memories of all our experiences, past and present, are stored internally within us. In psychological terms, these 'memories' have been defined as 'schemas'. You must 'unpack' all of the schemas that may be causing you emotional baggage, as these can manifest physically as illnesses. You do not need to judge these schemas, just observe and accept them.
- The actual cause of a past event/situation may be disproportionate to the emotional response that you attach to its memory.
- Your spiritual side must observe your mind, become aware of its response, and experience it without any judgement, to lessen the emotional baggage and improve your karmic position.
- The human species is comprised of spiritual beings in their human form, which includes the 'ego' (mind), our greatest challenge. The true you is not the thoughts and feelings that you experience in your human form.
- Our inner truth, which comes from our centre, should guide all of our thoughts and actions, rather than our human thoughts attempting to tell us the 'truth'.
- We are born with everything we need within us. Once you have your individually tailored tools and

techniques, your spiritual journey plays out internally between your true, higher self, and your 'rascal' ego (mind).

- The most painful emotional experiences represent the greatest opportunities for self-growth. 'Transformation comes from ruin!' (*Eat, Pray, Love* 2010).
- You *chose* this life, including your parents, depending on the lessons that you need to learn in this lifetime. Your parents also chose you (but don't own you).
- We are all here to learn our own specific lessons to balance karma in all directions in the fullness of time over all of our lifetimes. If you do not learn the lesson, 'opportunities for growth/developmental opportunities' will continue to reoccur until you *do* learn the lesson. I believe that if you do not learn a lesson in this lifetime, it will be carried over to your next lifetime/s to be learned in whatever form you are reincarnated.
- Addiction can **only** be dealt with by the individual concerned.
- If your focus in life is on your spiritual development, avoiding excessive use of vices, then your spiritual development/connection with the Source (universal love) will continue as part of a lifelong process.
- A balanced life with everything in moderation is acceptable and will not detract from your spiritual growth. The impact of a 'vice'/addiction is dependent on the power the individual has given it and on their 'true' intention.

- Humans who knowingly alter their consciousness by any means while opening doorways to the spiritual world do so at their own risk. This will play out through karma too. The power of the spiritual world should be respected and never underestimated.
- If you do not love yourself, you cannot love anyone else.
- 'Happiness' is defined as peace and contentment—inner harmony. Western cultures' teachings that wealth/money, accumulation of material possessions, achievement, and success will all lead to 'happiness' are untrue. Humans collectively need to unlearn what we've been taught through an 'awakened' education system. The Source's higher purpose for each of us is love and happiness.
- To further qualify, 'happiness' is about the journey, not just the destination! Without the lows/challenges, you would not appreciate the highs/good times. Too many people attempt to 'wrap themselves up in cotton wool' so as to never experience any pain or discomfort. You've attracted the pain anyway, so learn to sit in it (because if it doesn't kill you, it will make you stronger!).
- Everything is abundant; only humans conceive the term 'scarcity'. We are creative spiritual beings who are only constrained by our limited human mindsets.
- Be careful what you wish for; if your thoughts and actions (head and heart's desires) are aligned, your

wish will come true. You may not be aware of all of its implications. And is it aligned with the 'true' you?

- You may ask the Source what your true 'calling' is in this life. If we all worked in our passion, we would not consider it work. We all have unique, natural gifts and talents to contribute to this world.
- The more that you give, the more you will receive. You do not need material items, a house, security, employment, and money to live according to the natural order of things. In fact, all of these terms were conceived of by humans and do not exist in the spiritual realm.
- No living thing needs to suffer ongoing pain in this lifetime. If you do not allow the thought of such suffering to even enter your mind, it cannot manifest itself in your destiny. Your state of mind determines your 'happiness'. 'Pleasure, comfort, and happiness are a birthright' (Sophie Marsh, Nia Dance Instructor, 2015). It is disheartening to witness the number of people who choose to live in misery, rather than face the fear of change/transformation.
- Compassion is the greatest form of love. However, you must cease being compassionate with someone if it is at the expense of your own self-respect and health. Compassion for yourself comes first.
- Revenge is in the hands of the Source. You only need to watch the movie *The Reverent* (2015) to learn this lesson. No matter how betrayed, hurt, or

unfairly treated you may feel, it is not your place to take revenge unless it comes through you from the Source. And trust me, no one can serve up revenge better than the Source itself. Leave it to karma!

"Unthinkingly good things can happen, even late in the game – it's such a surprise."
(Under the Tuscan Sun, 2004)

Individual Preferences to Spirituality and Religion

Humans access universal love differently; however, it is all the one universal Source—whether it's through Christianity, Buddhism, reiki, meditation, Indian yoga, numerology, invoking angels, clearing chakras, dancing, walking, or horoscopes. All methods access the same universal Source. Some humans need theoretical, intellectual, strict, prescribed traditions and teachings to tap into their true self initially. It is very simple (based on the breath) and we've overcomplicated it. However, it's all acceptable and represents an individual choice. Never prescribe the method to anyone else, and never criticise or judge another's spiritual development/progress.

If humans recognised spiritual development and the presence of the universal Source from birth as fundamental in Western civilisations, especially through its educational systems and teachings, we would naturally be more connected in the first place. Hence, we would not need so many different, complicated tools and techniques to access what comes as true, inherent, and intuitive within us.

While humans *access* universal love differently, we also *experience* this same source differently. For example, some experience through feeling/sensing, some through their physical bodies, some through visualisations, or through 'clear hearing'. Never prescribe or try to tell someone what their individual experience or spiritual gifts will be.

"Anyone who is great at anything does it for their own approval, not somebody else's." (Gil Grissom in CSI)

Connection through Universal Love

We have all already ***experienced*** our connectedness to the universal Source, it's just that you have probably overlooked it. Reflect on how you feel at the birth of a new baby, or the electric atmosphere felt amongst the crowd at the Sydney 2000 Olympics, or when a butterfly flutters in your face on a walk. It was a defining moment for me when I discovered that this connection has been proven to exist scientifically and physically, even though we cannot define the basic energy source. What more proof do we need? For example, how does a newborn baby left on its mother's stomach straight out of the womb know to crawl its way to the nipple to feed? Or how do birds flying in a flock know which direction to travel in and when to change so they continue to fly in unison?

*"Africa is full of contradictions –
so beautiful, yet so cruel"
(Australian Idol in Africa).*

Negativity Trend Developing

The power of energy is, in simple terms, that we attract back whatever we put out to the universe. All living things sense every thought, emotion, and feeling emitted into the universe, so we need to be more mindful of what we put out there. While I am a big supporter of freedom of information and against any form of censorship, I would strongly argue that some information we put out into the universe does not serve humanity at all. For example, the beheading of a United Kingdom journalist by terrorists, which is published for all to see on the Internet. How does this serve anyone, especially his son who is alive today?

There is a disturbing trend developing; we are collectively putting more negative energy out there instead of positive energy. Consider the news reports every day, which are predominantly negative. Negativity feeds more negativity. As we become more separated from the Source, we focus more on unimportant things, creating realities with our human ego minds that only exist in this lifetime and that only serve to distract us spiritually.

Our forefathers would argue that the characteristics of competitiveness, war, aggression, and violence are all innate qualities in humans, resulting in this negative trend. This does not ring true, however, when you consider that animals and children are still connected to the Source. Most wild animals in nature will cooperate and live harmoniously together. For example, lions hunt in packs and only kill and take what they need for survival. Whereas, humans have been conditioned to be superior, greedy, and consumers in a capitalist society, taking a lot more than we need to live. Competition, conflict, war—characteristics adopted by our forefathers—are not innate or what comes naturally to humans. Love, compassion, and cooperation are innate qualities that we need to express and promote individually to hopefully bring about the necessary cultural change required to sustain human life on this planet.

As well as society adopting new values, it needs to remove societal expectations and reprioritise what is important. At a funeral, relatives will recognise the relationships with other living things that the deceased held, rather than what they achieved at work. As a society, we need to value traditionally feminine characteristics: nurturing, caring, compassion, cooperation, love—not competition, war, and conflict. (Then watch women break through the glass ceiling and be promoted into senior positions, instead of having to adopt masculine characteristics to compete in male-dominated workplaces!) The resulting realities manifested in the future would enable human existence to be more aligned with our spiritual beings. Consider this: if every human fulfilled their higher purpose, it probably would not be considered work. And the need for money may disappear as each person performed their passion.

So, try to get your head around the fact that our concepts of things such as governments, borders, nationalities, economy, money, war, airline disasters, conspiracies, trivia, academia, professions/careers, animal cruelty, and serial killers are all created constructs that only exist in the human form through the ego-mind. If we do not give them energy, they will cease to exist. What we think of and focus on today will manifest itself tomorrow if we can harness the true power of energy!

Enlightened individuals are conscientious when putting thoughts/energy into the universe, as they understand that they will attract back everything they put out. I used to think it was better to express your true feelings, even if they were negative, than to put on a false positive front. But as hard and trying as it has been, I have learned to transform negative feelings into positive as I began to understand the power of energy. "Fake it, until you make it!"

While we need to become more responsible, to only put positive energy out into the universe, we also need to be mindful not to give our attention to or witness negative energy put out by other human beings. Consider how much humans are multiplying negativity through the uncontrolled content published on the Internet alone. The Internet is a resource where any non-credible author can publish, which transcends national borders and can reach the world's population instantaneously. Then consider that that information can then be further copied, edited, sent, and stored. Once a thought has been conceived, it can manifest itself in our future.

"The hardest thing you can do is smile when you are ill, in pain, or depressed. But this no-cost remedy is a necessary first half-step if you are to start on the road to recovery."
(Allen Klein, azquotes.com)

Technological Advancements – More of a Hindrance

Unfortunately, capitalist societies have defined human progress through economic and technological advancements only. Humans are considered to be consumers rather than loving, spiritual beings.

Without understanding or being awakened to the natural order of things, humans have collectively developed technologies/architecture that only serve to separate us from nature and other living things, lessening our sacred connection. The information-rich society we live in and need for achievement and success means we're thinking and doing more rather than feeling and just being.

The Source wants us all to **experience** its joy, which is equivalent to universal joy. We are designed to be happy where everything is abundant. We create our own reality, as we have been given the freedom to make our own choices, and this is why we have been reincarnated in this human form in this lifetime. The Source does not want you to just preach about universal joy or read books about it. How can you **experience** universal joy through the technologies, architecture, workplaces, and mechanical vehicles we have created? I would argue these considered 'advancements' only serve to separate us from the Source. Pleasure, comfort, and happiness are a right!

People argue that the technologies themselves are not evil, but rather it's the users of the technologies that are evil. However, I beg to differ. The sacred connection that should guide us is lessened when you consider that technologies physically separate us from other living things. We should all be able to put space between our thoughts, as well as feel and connect to all living things. Societal expectations, rules/laws, cultures, created constructs, technologies, and architecture should all support and facilitate our species' advancement and this sacred connection.

Humans are not living in this world, nor on this planet, the way we are meant to spiritually. We cannot sustain human life on this planet unless we change the way we live and adopt new values, as we are literally destroying our environment and beyond.

"If a child smiles, if an adult smiles, that is very important. If in our daily lives we can smile, if we can be peaceful and happy, not only we, but everyone will profit from it … Our smile affirms our awareness and determination to live in peace and joy. The source of a true smile is an awakened mind." (Thich Nhat Hanh)

Basis of Meditation

Meditation and self-love are essential to a human's health and wellbeing and these concepts should be mandated daily across all Western schools and workplaces. The Dalai Lama states in *Qigong is a Way of Being*, 'If every eight-year-old in the world is taught meditation, we would eliminate violence from the world within one generation.' If I could have my way, all computers and classes/workplaces would observe a 'quiet time' at the same time for 20 minutes every day for the practice of meditation. While no one can enforce people to meditate during this time, at least this would provide a supportive, quiet environment without the usual distractions.

The practice of meditation is learning how to discipline and quieten the mind. Profound changes take place within you when you undertake this practice regularly. The simplest way to commence meditation is through focusing on your breath. Observe that your body is breathing in, and your body is breathing out. After counting to achieve the same length of breath with your inhalation and exhalation, attempt to 'put space between your thoughts' by holding your breath in after the inhalation, and holding it out after your exhalation. This requires some practice to master.

The art of meditation comes more easily to some people than others. Some people may naturally be meditating without even realising they are doing it!

Others may instantly feel an inner peace that comes from meditation from the first time they are taught. Unfortunately, this was not the case for me. Being at the lowest point in my life and with nothing to lose, I made myself conduct a guided meditation by listening to a CD for 20 minutes every morning for six months. Then I started to feel the benefits. I cannot tell you how painfully difficult this was to enforce when I was not experiencing any of the benefits initially. There was no instant gratification. While I don't need to adopt such a structured approach to meditation nowadays, I have identified that some form of regular meditation is essential to my health and wellbeing.

"The universe is conspiring in our favour, always and in all ways."
(Neale Donald Walsch,
Conversations with God)

Can Women Have It All in This Day and Age?

This is an equivalent question for men too. The short answer is yes, as we are creative, spiritual beings who can create our own reality. This may be easier said than done … you just have to change the way you think!

It's challenging to unlearn everything you have been taught, to rewire your mind by developing new behaviour patterns so that new mental pathways can be formed. It's very difficult to think outside the norm, given the expectations, traditions, laws and rules, teachings, education systems, and adopted values of today's Western civilisations. Currently, we do not even have the language to describe the new 'landscape' we are capable of creating. Meditation and recording your dreams to determine common themes can help you tap into your unconscious and assist with changing the way you think. The more self-love you grow through connecting with the Source, the harder it becomes to live life the way our society expects us to.

What a profoundly different world it would be if all humans remained connected to the Source and were taught the value of self-esteem throughout our lives. I would argue that most if not all personal issues, once broken down, centre on a lack of self-love and low self-esteem.

People like me who become separated from the Source at a young age would benefit from having these universal principles ingrained from childhood. Otherwise, they risk losing the identity of their real self entirely. Our minds tend to be consumed predominantly with thinking, meaning that over time, we become more desensitised to our feelings, which we've been conditioned to shut down anyway.

I recently heard the saying, 'Returning to where you were is not the same as knowing you never left.' In truth, we are always connected to the Source, it's just our perception of connection that may have become severed. These universal principles are an attempt to convert the natural order of things scientifically through theory and proof for those of us who have been conditioned to think predominantly with the left-hand side of our brain. This is so the majority of us who have lost our perceived connection and only experience thinking (never feeling) can digest it using our conditioned minds. As I have worked out, happiness for me is defined as inner harmony. Unfortunately, I spent almost forty years believing that it was achieved through success, work, career, qualifications, marriage, children, partying, sex, drugs, rock and roll, excess, and consumption. So, the question is, would meeting society's expectations in terms of career, marriage, children, house, and investments bring you inner harmony and joy? If life is all about our personal journey and all that really matters is how you feel about yourself, and if no one else knows why you chose this path and what your higher purpose is in this lifetime, then how can they judge whether you achieved what you were sent here to do?

There is no way that I could (or would want to) raise children, fulfil a career, or maintain a marriage and household in this day and age and still be able to find inner peace within myself! Who said we need to work five days a week from 9 am to 5 pm, to travel in peak-hour traffic to air-conditioned, concrete jungles where we cannot even open a window, and then sit behind a computer screen for over seven and a half hours every day? It seems ludicrous, doesn't it?

I also question whether I would want to bring up children in a world where they cannot just *be* innocent children. Children today are exposed to so much misinformation and have to abide by meaningless laws and rules, which would be unnecessary if we all lived according to the natural order. They cannot even run under a sprinkler, given today's water restrictions, and the good old firecracker night has been banned forever!

While I was a very staunch feminist twenty years ago, strongly believing that a woman could do anything that a man could do, including fighting on the frontline of a warzone, I have entirely reversed my view. Some women do have the physical capability to do everything a man can do. However, physiologically speaking, men and women's bodies are designed differently for a different intended purpose. I now believe that traditional gender roles have been designed for a reason and that men and women are meant to complement each other.

Men and women should not both be working full-time, while childcare workers are raising their children.

Just Being

Especially when you consider that values are ingrained in children up until the age of six years old. This represents quality bonding time between a parent and their child. I believe the Source intended a child only be conceived naturally as the product and pinnacle of an intimately mature relationship between a man and a woman. The couple would know and love themselves and each other unconditionally and their relationship would be solid and enduring based on love, respect, trust, and openness. There is no greater role than raising a child where a person has as much influence over the life of a pure, innocent, untouched child.

My existence certainly needed to be more aligned with my spiritual development as, at the time, I was contributing to the manufacture of weapons for war. So, I quit the job that I had worked at for over twenty-two years. If you are enlightened and truly trust in these universal principles, you do not need a backup plan or be fearful and maintain a safety net as an employee. **If you have the faith and trust to pursue your higher purpose, then, in turn, you will *experience* true, universal joy.** The more you give, the more you receive. You simply cannot lose! Oh, how logical the natural order is!

I'm not suggesting that people should quit their job and rely on the universe to provide for them. Responsibility comes with spiritual development. However, every problem can be resolved by working with the Source. Much of what I've spoken about in the spiritual realm is intangible, so you have to have a blind faith to believe. As stated earlier, the Source takes care of the 'how', which we rarely comprehend with our limited human minds. So, we just need to be clear on what we expect and express our gratitude for it, and the Source will take care of the rest.

"Balance is not letting anybody love you less than you love yourself."
(Eat, Pray, Love)

Relationships Today

Of all the relationships that I personally know of, I could honestly count on one hand what I consider to be the number of good relationships and marriages. Too many people enter into relationships without ever truly knowing and loving themselves. We are taught that you cannot love anyone else unless you love yourself, and yet, so many people enter into relationships without ever feeling content and complete within themselves. I know many people who are in unhealthy, co-dependent relationships and are too fearful to leave them. I have friends in loveless marriages who have exit strategies in place for when their children finish school!

The kind of relationship I desire is one where two spiritual beings come together. This is not to say that the relationship would be perfect—we are still human after all. However, this relationship would be loving and respectful always and one would accept and adore the other person as they are, without ever judging or criticising them. I have defined to myself the qualities of my ideal relationship, although I do question whether we are meant to be monogamous. To think you will grow at the same pace and in the same direction with the same person over your entire lifetime is questionable. The truth is that you undertake a lot more self-growth when you are on your own and only have yourself to focus on. Although, I do believe we are social beings who are meant to experience life and share the world with someone.

*"We could spend our lives
together miserable. But be happy
not to be apart!"*
(Eat, Pray, Love)

Rewiring Our Mind and Overcoming Addictions/Unproductive Behaviour Patterns

Addictions are habits or learned behaviour patterns that the individual keeps repeating. So little is understood about the human brain and its functioning. Apparently, humans only use 10 per cent of their brains! As brain cells can regenerate (beyond our early twenties as once thought) we can change the way we think and develop mind-muscle at any age.

Once you comprehend that you are what you think and you attract what you put out into the universe, you can start to harness the power of energy and truly create your own reality.

The brain's ability to regenerate neurons is called 'neurogenesis' and is accelerated through steroid hormones, which are stimulated through physical activity. Hence, healthy brain functioning requires physical exercise, mental activities such as meditation, and brain exercises. This further highlights the importance of a holistic approach to maintaining human health and wellbeing, which integrates the body, mind, and spirit.

Recent studies conducted by Dr Libby Weaver, Australia's leading nutritional biochemist, have shown that the only way to access a restorative place for our lifeforce is through extending the length of our exhalation (holding our breath out after exhaling)—the basis of meditation. Dr Weaver has found that when taking shallow breaths, our bodies think we're in danger. Operating in fight-or-flight mode causes our bodies to access our glucose rather than our fat stores for energy, leading to us feeling more tired and gaining weight.

"The body is the barometer of the soul." (Annette Noontil, 1994)

We Can Heal Ourselves

I believe that ailments, illnesses, diseases, and skin conditions are all a reflection of what's occurring internally. Any unresolved emotional baggage will manifest itself physically within the individual. As stated earlier, when broken down, most people's issues will centre on a lack of self-love, originating in their childhood and involving the parents they chose in this lifetime. The more serious the illness, the more deeply ingrained the issues causing it. Unfortunately, much of modern Western medicine today generally only treats the symptoms, not the cause of the condition. This may result in perpetuating the cause, rather than solving it.

The key may lie in monitoring the ph levels within our bodies, as apparently viruses, bacteria, and fungi cannot live in an alkaline environment. So even if we contract an external bug, it will be ineffectual and unable to harm us if we maintain a strong immune system achieved through a balanced internal terrain. Consistent with the universal principles, nothing has any power over us unless we allow it!

I believe that all of the answers and solutions we seek lie within us and in the nature that we are connected to. We should be more conscious of our human footprint and its implications on nature's cycles. Until we better understand this, humans should try to be less imposing. We do not even know what the appendix within our bodies was designed for. I find it hard to believe that scientists think the presence of our appendix could be a design fault leftover from our species' evolution.

My mother taught me—in support of me consuming a lot of water daily—to consider the inner workings of my body as similar to a running stream. You want your stream crystal clear and free-flowing, not dirty, blocked, dried up, or stagnant. It seems logical when you consider that we regularly monitor the ph levels of water in a fish tank to maintain the fish and marine life. Yet, humans rarely consider our individual ph levels, even given the fact that our bodies are composed of about 70 per cent water. Interestingly, more than 70 per cent of the Earth's surface is covered in water. Coincidence? I think not!

We should be paying closer attention to lunar cycles too. The moon's gravitational pull can affect our body's water levels, similarly to the oceans' tides. Women even menstruate according to lunar cycles! If a healthy woman's natural cycle has not been distracted, which is less defined today, she will bleed during the dark phase of the moon (New Moon). A person can experience decreased physical and mental energy levels during the New Moon when there is a strong downward flowing energy in the universe. This could have a much broader application, even with scheduling exercise classes!

I believe that humans should be living more in tune with nature. For example, we should be sleeping more during the winter months when the days are shorter and colder.

Did you know that Mother Nature has even created fruit and vegetables in the shape of the human organ that they assist? For example, avocadoes, which are shaped like a womb, are good for pregnancy. Nuts such as walnuts shaped liked an iris are good for your eyes. Every living thing has been designed with a purpose in mind and is intended to operate as an integral part of a complex, interconnected whole.

Doctors should be examining patients holistically—you cannot separate mind, body, and spirit. Swiss Psychologist Carl Jung has already proven that a person's level of spiritual convictions determines their level of psychosis/neurosis (Seamon and Kenrick, c1994). Through restoring someone's spiritual beliefs, you can improve their condition mentally and physically. No wonder there is a growing market for alternative and naturopathic medicine and treatments.

I was horrified to discover that my doctor's first response to my claim of depression was to prescribe anti-depressants without even enquiring into my well-being, mental health, stress levels, sleep patterns, diet, drug use, work habits/pressures, exercise, and relationships. Consider these days how children labelled as hyperactive are medicated with Ritalin (equivalent to 'speed'), without any research being conducted into the long-term effects of this drug on their physical development in later life. Hyperactivity is not a new condition; it has always existed. It's just that we've come up with new labels for it, such as ADHD, and medications to address the symptoms.

The importance placed on mental health and on preserving our brain functioning should become even more evident when you consider that we are what we think, and as creative beings we need to be able to tame and discipline our rascal ego minds. Without control of our minds, we are unable to direct our destiny. Our spiritual being within our centre should be controlling our mind's thoughts. And I believe a key to achieving this is through listening to your body and making small, ongoing tweaks based on your experiences of pleasure versus pain. If you are centred and grounded, your body can act as a powerful indicator of your higher, spiritual self, if you listen and respond to its sensory intelligence.

Some issues that society is facing today are very complex but do serve to highlight the interconnectedness between seemingly separate variables. For example, there has been an increase in the number of people suffering from thyroid problems. This is because we are not getting the iodine that used to be found naturally in soil due to its degradation. This is an environmental problem that humans have caused, which is resulting in increased health problems for us (karma!). As Sir Isaac Newton discovered, 'every action has an equal and opposite reaction'. (Oh, the natural order!)

While I believe I have a high pain threshold, I would refuse to live with ongoing, chronic pain. People with terminal illnesses have attracted their condition in some way and are internally (whether they're conscious of it or not) allowing it to continue, which no one likes to hear. The solutions to all human health and medical problems lie within us, or the nature that we are connected to. We could heal ourselves if we better understood our design and intended purpose, which would be instinctive if we were guided by the universal force.

Human health and medical problems may be caused by developing an emotional attachment to a person, place, or thing, which leads to us feeling fearful over its potential loss. Any emotional baggage that isn't observed, acknowledged, and released will only manifest itself physically over time. Unfortunately, a 'one-size-fits-all' approach cannot be applied, as the condition and its treatment will depend on the individual.

As modern Western medicine attempts to separate a person's physical ailments from their internal realities, it typically only treats the symptoms and not the cause. However, I am not dismissing the benefits of Western medicine and believe in order to truly heal yourself, you should be willing to investigate every possibility: Western and alternative medicine.

"Our moral responsibility is not to stop the future, but to shape it ... to channel our destiny in humane directions and to try to ease the trauma of transition."
(Alvin Toffler in Criminal Minds)

No Such Thing as 'Death'

There is no such thing as death, as our spirit and soul are eternal and live on beyond this life. Our human body, however, which is the vessel for our soul/spirit in this lifetime, does not exist beyond this life. Nor is there a heaven and hell beyond this lifetime, as we will continue to live on in another form in another time. The closest we will get to heaven or hell is through the realities humans create for themselves here on Earth.

Similarly, past evil personalities such as Hitler, Saddam Hussein, and Bin Laden are all part of the same universal source. Only humans assign values to things and judge accordingly. The Source is pure love and only knows pure love. I believe this is why humans were created so that the Source could experience itself. This would not be possible without contrast, values, and judgement.

*"A man's richness is measured
by the fewest of his needs."
(Wayne Dyer)*

Integrity and Resilience

Integrity and resilience are the two qualities I most admire in humans. It makes sense that aligning your actions with your core values will make you feel better about yourself, which I believe is the most important thing in life.

Integrity is about doing what you think is right, regardless of whether you think anyone is watching you. Desirably, what you consider to be 'right' should align with your eternal true self, which is equivalent to the universal truth.

Resilience is the quality of being able to bounce back in the face of setbacks. It is the strength to endure, which will lead to happiness when you consider that happiness is about the journey, not the destination. You cannot appreciate something without experiencing its opposite too. For example, we would not know the sensation of pleasure if we did not feel the sensation of pain, or good without bad, or right without wrong, or light without dark.

Self-transformation (or 'self-realisation' defined as experiencing what we already know) is not a one-off event that occurs in our life. It is a lifelong process where after learning a lesson we are presented with another opportunity for spiritual growth.

There is a strong, innate drive within me to be happy and attain this right of mine. I struggle to comprehend people who are miserable but choose to remain this way out of fear. I would rather not be living than to be living feeling miserable and not to be true to myself. That's the definition of hell on Earth for me!

References

Australian Idol in Africa, The Finale, Season 3, Episode 53.

Byrne, R. (c2006). *The Secret*. New York: Atria Books and Oregon: Beyond Words Publishing.

Conversations with God. [fiche]. 2006. Directed by Stephen Simon.

Criminal Minds, 'The Boys of Sudworth Place', Season 10, Episode 8.

Dead Poets Society. [fiche]. 1989. Touchstone Pictures and Silver Screen Partners IV.

Dyer, W. Facebook/Dr. Wayne Dyer's Teachings.

Dyer, W.W. (2005). *You'll See It When You Believe It*. London: Arrow Books.

Eat, Pray, Love. [fiche], 2010. Colombia Pictures.

Foundation for Inner Peace. (c2007). *A Course in Miracles*. Combined Volume. 3rd edn. California: Foundation for Inner Peace.

Grissom, G. *CSI*, 'Execution of Catherine Willows', Season 3, Episode 6.

Hanh, T.N. *Thich Nhat Hanh Quote Collective*, thichnhathanhquotecollective.com.

Hay, L.L. (c1984). *You Can Heal Your Life*. Carlsbad, California: Hay House.

Hamilton, M. (2009). *The Magic of the Moment*. Victoria: Penguin Group (Australia).

McMillen, K. and McMillen, A. (2014). *When I Loved Myself Enough*. New South Wales: Pan Macmillan Australia.

Meyer, J. (c2004). *Ending Your Day Right*. New York: Faith Words.

Meyer, J. (c2004). *Starting Your Day Right*. New York: Faith Words.

Noontil, A. (1994). *The Body is the Barometer of the Soul: So be Your Own Doctor II*. Australia: Lucienne Noontil.

Satir, V.M. (c1975). *Self-esteem*. California: Celestial Arts.

Seamon, J.G. and Kenrick, D.T. (c1994). *Psychology.* 2nd edn. New Jersey: Prentice-Hall.

The Revenant. [fiche], 2015. Appian Way.

Tolle, E. (2004). *The power of now: a guide to spiritual enlightenment.* New South Wales: Hachette Australia.

Weaver, L. (2015). Studio 10, 'Why We Feel So Tired', https://youtu.be/Ir09Amhnxtk.

Walsch, N.D. (c1995). *Conversations with God: An Uncommon Dialogue, Book 1.* New South Wales: Hachette Australia.

Williamson, M. (c1994). *Illuminata: A Return to Prayer.* New York: Penguin Group (USA).

About the Author

Joanna Button, BComm, GradCertComm (Defence), GradDipOrgComm, MAOrgComm

From selling kebabs and VIP Pies, to acting as a gymnastics coach, a naturopath receptionist, and a fashion store manager, the pinnacle of Joanna's career would have to be as the Media Adviser to the Chief of Navy. On call 24/7, Joanna was responsible for upholding Navy's reputation, which was a bit of a long shot given it was comprised of roughly 20,000 Navy members and fifty commissioned vessels at the time.

It must have felt like going round the buoy again, as for nine years while Joanna worked full-time, she studied part-time to complete her graduate certificate, graduate diploma, and then masters in communication through Charles Sturt University.

After flying colours in the communication and media field, Joanna then obtained qualifications in business continuity management and managed the Defence executive's business continuity program including 'wargaming' its plan. Representing Defence in an interagency working group saw Joanna contribute to ensuring the continuity of government in the event of a business disruption affecting the Governor General and/or the Prime Minister.

Just Being

As a dog lover and owner, Joanna lives in Australia's Capital Territory with her Irish Wolfhound named Grover (previously Conker) and Australian Terrier cross named Teacup. Joanna is passionate about justice, equality, and the truth, of which there is only one version.

www.ingramcontent.com/pod-product-compliance
Lightning Source LLC
Chambersburg PA
CBHW020301010526
44108CB00037B/510